Five
Black Bears

HOW SCIENTISTS COUNT ALASKA'S ANIMALS

Photographs & text by Harriet McClain

FISH BONE STUDIO   SITKA, ALASKA

One way scientists study and learn
about plants and animals is by counting them.
During the summer, this researcher lives
on a small remote island in Alaska,
counting and studying birds.

1
orca

Sometimes orcas leap all the way out of the water, this is called breaching. An adult orca can be 26 feet in length and weigh over 6 tons. That's a big splash! When they are not upside down like this one, orcas can be counted and identified by their tall dorsal fins and the black and white patches on their backs.

2
ravens

Ravens are very smart birds. They can solve problems.
Scientists have shown that they can remember people
and places. The annual Christmas bird count in
Prudhoe Bay, Alaska is easy. There is usually only 1 kind
of bird to count. The only bird that can survive
the 40 degree below zero weather is the raven.

3
sea otters

Sea otters spend their entire lives in the cold
Pacific Ocean. Their thick fur keeps them warm.
Sea otters use rocks as tools to open hard clamshells.
For years scientists found very few sea otters
to count in Alaska. By counting and studying sea otters,
scientists have found ways to help the sea otter
return to Southeast Alaska.

4
harbor
seals

Harbor seals spend part of every day out of
the water. Sometimes they haul out on rocky shores,
and sometimes on icebergs. Although these 2 pups
are large, they are less than 2 weeks old.
The pups were able to swim and dive just hours
after they were born. Scientists use computers
to follow and study harbor seals. Some seals have
been given radio satellite tags that show how far
and where the seals have traveled.

5 black bears

Black bears gather every summer at this creek to catch salmon. They spend the winter sleeping in their dens, living on the body fat they made by eating so many salmon. Scientists can use bear hair to help count how many black bears are in an area. Wire snags capture the bear's hair as it passes by, like hair in a hairbrush. Then scientists use DNA and other markers found in the hair to identify and count the bears.

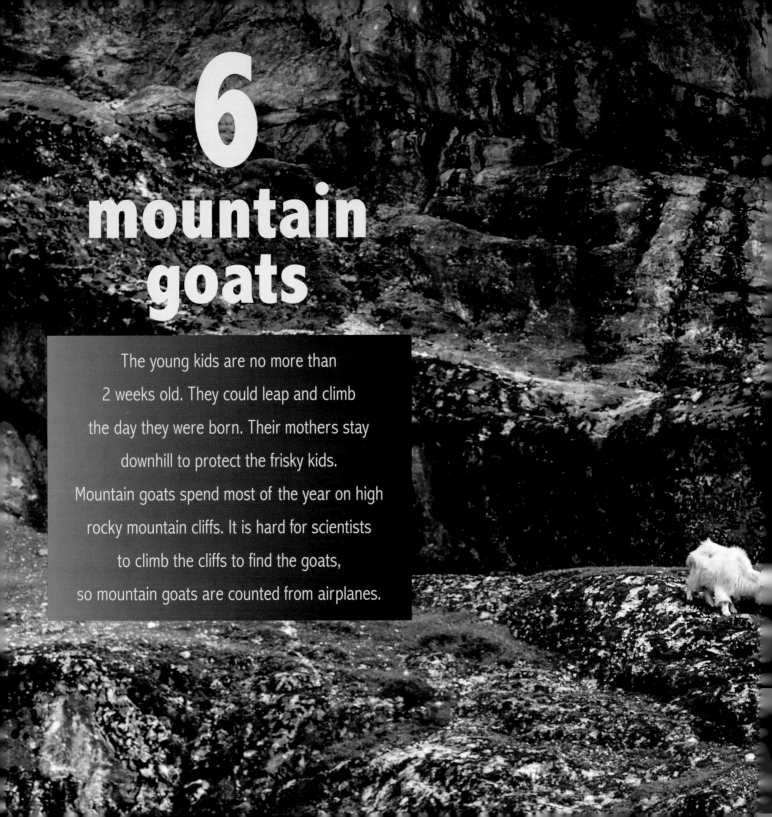

6
mountain
goats

The young kids are no more than
2 weeks old. They could leap and climb
the day they were born. Their mothers stay
downhill to protect the frisky kids.
Mountain goats spend most of the year on high
rocky mountain cliffs. It is hard for scientists
to climb the cliffs to find the goats,
so mountain goats are counted from airplanes.

7
slugs

The largest slug in North America, the Pacific banana slug, is found in the rain forests of Southeast Alaska. They can reach 10 inches in length. Top speed for a slug this size is 30 feet an hour. Scientists who study slugs can count the number of slugs in a small area, then use math to estimate how many slugs are in a large area.

8
brown bears

It is unusual to see a mother bear with 4 cubs. There are 3 young cubs on the rock and the fourth small cub is in the river. The 2 larger, older cubs on the rock with the salmon bits are probably a year old. Their mother is close by. All the bears are at this stream to eat as many salmon as they can before winter. This is a lot of bears! Researchers count and study bears to find out how many bears will fish together at a salmon stream.

9
clams

Clams are bivalves. That means
they have a 2 part shell, where
2 valves make 1 clam.
Many times only 1 part of the clam
is found. Here all the butter clams
and heart cockles have both parts
of their shells still connected.

10
bear claws

Brown bears have long claws that help them
dig for roots, insects, small animals and clams,

11 Dungeness crab

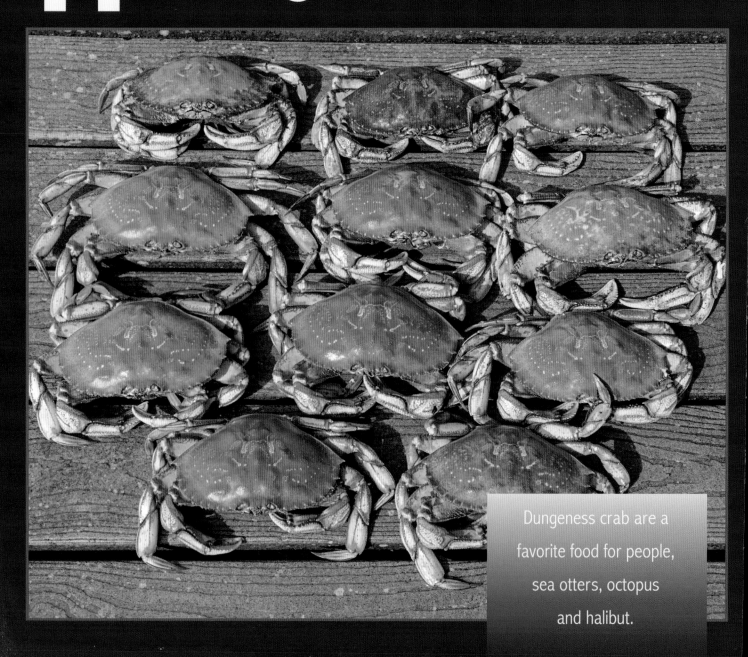

Dungeness crab are a favorite food for people, sea otters, octopus and halibut.

12 green shore crab

Turn over a rock at low tide on an outer coast beach to find tiny green shore crabs. Scientists have counted over 5,000 different kinds of crab around the world.

13
sea stars

The Pacific sea star is found on rocky
beaches from Alaska to Baja California.
If a sea star loses a leg, it can grow
a new one. Scientists are counting
sea stars to study the effects of warmer
temperatures on the sea stars and the other
creatures that live along the ocean shore.

14
salmonberries

Salmonberries are ripe and ready to pick in the late summer. People pick them to make jelly. Bears, ravens and other animals also eat salmonberries. Scientists count how many different kinds of plants and animals live together in the forest. This is called biodiversity. Scientists want to know how many kinds of berries are in the forest and how many bears are eating the berries.

15
puffins

Puffins dive for fish, holding up to 10 small fish in their bill at one time. The sharp nails on their webbed feet help them climb on rocky cliffs, where they can dig underground nests. Researchers count puffins every year at the same time in the same place so they can compare and study the numbers.

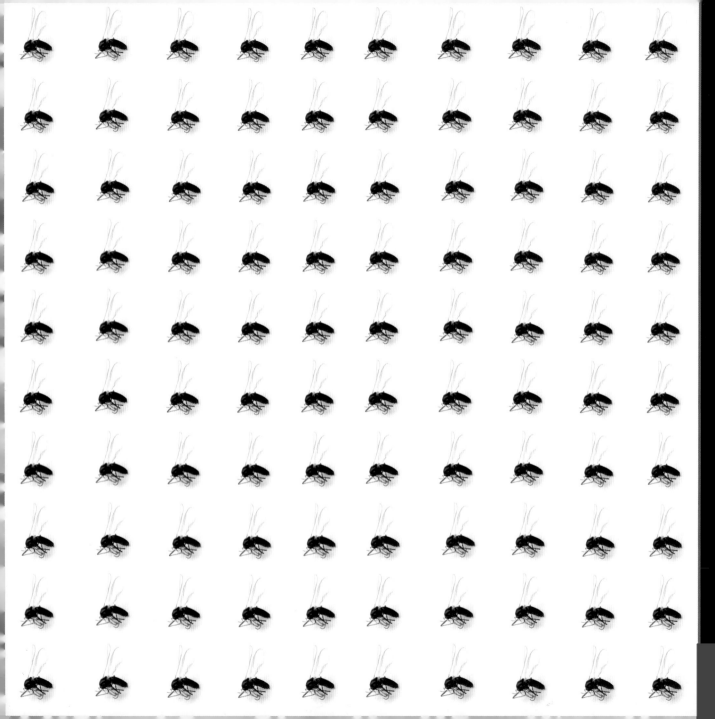

100
no seeums

You may not see it, but you will know if this tiny insect bites you. Your skin will itch for weeks.
Entomologists are scientists who study insects and they have a big job! Entomologists
estimate that at any given time there are 10 quintillion (10,000,000,000,000,000,000)
individual insects alive. Only half of the different kinds of insect species have been
described and named by scientists. You could discover a new insect species.

How many Steller sea lions?

The really big Steller sea lions are males. They can weigh 1200 pounds or more. They make a roaring noise like a lion. These sea lions use this rocky stretch of shore as a haulout for several weeks each summer.

In between trips out into the ocean to get food, they rest here. Scientists using spoons scrape sea lion poop off the rocks to learn what the sea lions have been eating.

Keep counting.

Scientists count Steller sea lions by flying over the haulout and taking photos. On the photo they put a dot on each sea lion. Computer software counts the dots. By using a photo, only the sea lions that were resting on the rocks can be counted.

What about the sea lions who are out in the ocean getting food? How will the scientists count them? Biometricians are scientists who use math to find ways to answer questions like this. To count all the sea lions, a few are marked so they can be easily counted in the photos.

Scientists figure out how many marked sea lions are missing and can then estimate how many other sea lions are out at sea. In some areas the number of Steller sea lions has been getting smaller. Scientists are counting and studying to find out why.

Either way, keep counting.

Scientists count animals and plants to see how healthy the planet is. If the number of Steller sea lions or puffins or slugs is changing, scientists study the animal, trying to learn what the problem is. Scientists count and study to make sure there will be enough fish,

berries, birds and bears for the future.
As a volunteer at events like the Christmas bird
count you can help scientists count animals.
Or maybe you want to go to school to become
a biologist, a scientist who studies and
counts plants and animals.

A big thank you to everyone who gave support and expertise to this project

Keeara Rhoades at Photo Center Northwest, Seattle pcnw.org

Victoria O'Connell, Sitka Sound Science Center, SitkaScience.org

Brenda Schwartz-Yeager, Wrangell bear guide, AlaskaUpClose.com

Les and Evie Kinnear, FortressOfTheBear.org, Sitka

The Staff aboard The Baranof Dream, AlaskaDreamCruises.com

Rose Michelle Taverniti, graphic artist

Ron McClain, crab wrangler, boat captain and Alaska wildlife expert

Alaska Department of Fish and Game and their great web site about animals and animal research, www.adfg.alaska.gov

© FishBone Studio 2013

Photographs © 2013 Harriet McClain

Book Design, Rose Michelle Taverniti

Fish Bone Studio, PO Box 66, Sitka, Alaska 99835

Printed by Everbest Printing Co., in Guangzhou, China through Alaska Print Brokers, Anchorage, Alaska.